Daily Zen
Quilts & Projects

by Melanie Greseth and Joanie Holton
for TailorMade by Design

Landauer Publishing, LLC

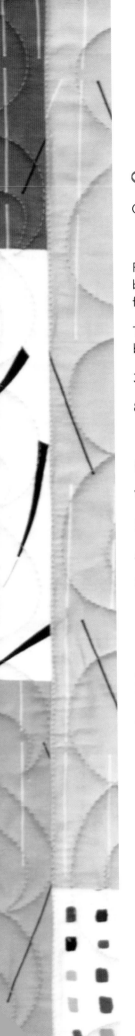

Daily Zen
Quilts & Projects

Projects Copyright © 2014
by Melanie Greseth and Joanie Holton
for TailorMade by Design

This book was designed, produced, and published
by Landauer Publishing, LLC

3100 101st Street, Urbandale, IA 50322

800-557-2144; 515-287-2144; landauerpub.com

President/Publisher: Jeramy Lanigan Landauer

Vice President of Sales and Administration: Kitty Jacobson

Editor: Jeri Simon

Art Director: Laurel Albright

Photographer: Sue Voegtlin

ISBN 13: 978-1-935726-60-9

Table of Contents

Introduction

Michele D'Amore's newest fabric collection, Daily Zen for Contempo Fabrics, features simple graphic images and a varied color palette. Our creative spirits were inspired. Zen emphasizes the value of meditation and focus. We have always found our greatest source of Zen in front of our sewing machines or with needle and thread in hand.

We hope you experience peace and contentment while creating the quilts and other projects in this book. The projects range from beginner to challenging intermediate, a bit of something for everyone.

Joanie and Melanie

Daily Zen

by Michele D'Amore

Pick Up Sticks-
grass green

Pick Up Sticks-royal

Pick Up Sticks-aqua

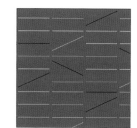

Pick Up Sticks-teal

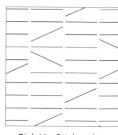

Pick Up Sticks-white

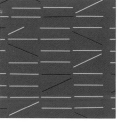

Pick Up Sticks-fuchsia

Pick Up Sticks-iris

Pick Up Sticks-gray

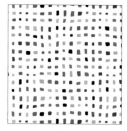

Zen Plaid-blue

Broadway
Texture-white on white

Zen Flower-dark taupe

Zen Flower-moss

Zen Flower-lilac

Zen Flower-white

Zen Flower-claret red

Zen Flower-
white on black

Quill-white

Quill-fuchsia

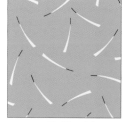

Quill-gold

Quill-split pea

Leaf-olive

Leaf-gray

Leaf-gray on white

Leaf-violet

Leaf-white

Unified Quilt

Finished quilt size – 64-1/2" x 72"

Yardage

2 yards black-on-white fabric

1 yard white fabric

1-1/4 yard grass green fabric

2-1/4 yards royal fabric

5 yards backing fabric

65" x 90" batting

WOF = width of fabric

Cutting

From the black-on-white fabric, cut:
(2) 13" x 25-1/2" J rectangles
(5) 13" E squares
(2) 9-7/8" x 13" M rectangles
(2) 9-7/8" x 25-1/2" N rectangles

From the white fabric, cut:
(3) 6-3/4" x 9-7/8" D rectangles
(4) 6-3/4" B squares
(3) 6-3/4" x 22-3/8" G rectangles

From the grass green fabric, cut:
(6) 4" squares; sub cut once on the diagonal to make 12 F triangles
(3) 3-5/8" x 22-3/8" I strips
(9) 3-5/8" x 9-7/8" A strips
(3) 3-5/8" x 25-1/2" H strips
(3) 3-5/8" x 13" C strips
(2) 3-5/8" x 6-3/4" L strips

From the royal fabric, cut:
(6) 4" squares; sub cut once on the diagonal to make 12 F triangles
(12) 3-5/8" x 9-7/8" A strips
(4) 7-1/2" x WOF side border strips
(4) 2" x WOF top and bottom border strips
(8) 2-1/4" x WOF binding strips

From the backing fabric, cut:
(2) 90" x WOF pieces

SEWING INSTRUCTIONS:

Making the Blocks

Framed Square Blocks

1. With top raw edges even, sew (1) green A strip to the left side of (1) B square. Sew with a 1/4" seam allowance, stopping 1/2" from the bottom of the B square. Press seam toward A.

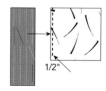

2. Sew (1) royal A strip to the top of the B square. Press seam toward A.

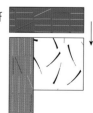 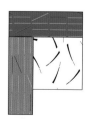

3. Sew (1) green A strip to the right side of the B square. Press seam toward A.

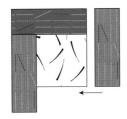

4. Sew (1) royal A strip to the bottom of the B square, moving the green strip aside to stitch the seam to the end of the bottom edge. Fold the beginning green A strip onto the block over the royal A strip, right sides together and matching the raw edges along the bottom. Sew to finish the seam and complete a Framed Square block. Make 2 Framed Square Blocks.

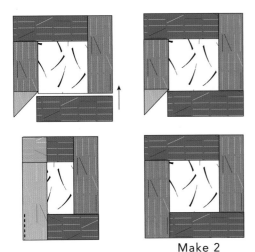

Make 2

Small 3-sided Framed Blocks

1. Sew (1) green L strip to the left side of (1) B square. Press seam toward L.

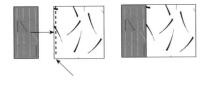

2. Sew (1) royal A strip to the top of the B square. Press seam toward A.

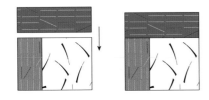

3. Sew (1) green A strip to the right side of the B square. Press seam toward A to complete a Small 3-sided Framed block. Make 2 Small 3-sided Framed Blocks.

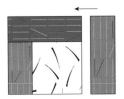

Make 2

Medium 3-sided Framed Blocks

1. Sew (1) green A strip to the top of (1) D rectangle. Press seam toward A.

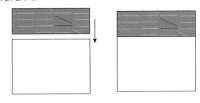

2. Sew (1) royal A strip to the right side of D rectangle. Press seam toward A.

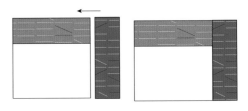

3. Sew (1) green C strip to the bottom of the D rectangle. Press seam toward C to make a Medium 3-sided Framed block. Make 3 Medium 3-sided Framed Blocks.

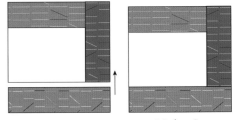

Make 3

Large 3-sided Framed Blocks

1. Sew (1) green I strip to the bottom of (1) G rectangle. Press seam toward I.

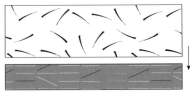

2. Sew (1) royal A strip to the left side of the G rectangle. Press seam toward A.

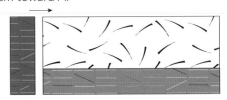

3. Sew (1) green H strip to the top of the G rectangle. Press seam toward H to make a Large 3-sided Framed block. Make 3 Large 3-sided Framed Blocks.

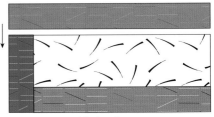

Make 3

Snowball Squares

You will use F triangles for ALL the snowball squares. On the wrong side of ALL F triangles, mark 1/4" seam line on the triangle base.

1. Mark 3-5/8" from each corner on the right side of (3) E squares.

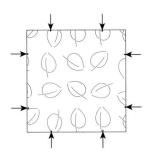

2. With right sides together, place (1) green F triangle in the corner of (1) E square. Match the seam lines on the base of the F triangle to the 3-5/8" marks on either edge of the E square corner, with the triangle pointing toward the center of the square.

3. Sew across the F triangle base on the marked seam allowance. Trim the excess E square fabric to match the triangle's seam allowance. Press the triangle back.

4. Repeat on the remaining corners of the E square. Square the block to 13" to make a Snowball Square. Make 3 Snowball Squares.

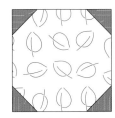

Make 3

Half Snowball Squares

Following the same process for making a snowball square, mark 3-5/8" from corners on the right edge of (2) E squares. Sew (1) royal F triangle on the upper and lower right corners of (1) E square. Square the block to 13" to make a Half Snowball Square. Make 2 Half Snowball Squares.

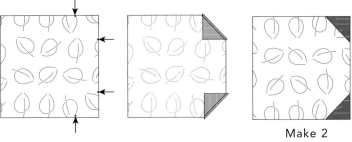

Make 2

Half Snowball Large Rectangles

Following the same process for making a snowball square, mark 3-5/8" from corners on the left edge of (2) J rectangles. Sew (1) royal F triangle on the upper and lower left corners of (1) J rectangle to make a Half Snowball Large Rectangle. Make 2 Half Snowball Large Rectangles.

Make 2

Small Single Snowball Corner

1. Following the same process for making a snowball square, mark 3-5/8" from corner on bottom right edge of (1) M rectangle. Sew (1) royal F triangle on the bottom right corner to make a Small Single Snowball Corner.

Make 1

2. Mark 3-5/8" from corner on top right edge of (1) M rectangle. Sew (1) royal F triangle on the top right corner to make a Small Single Snowball Corner.

Make 1

Single Snowball Corner Large Rectangle

1. Following the same process for making a snowball square, mark 3-5/8" from corner on bottom left edge of (1) N rectangle. Sew (1) royal F triangle on the bottom left corner to make a Single Snowball Corner Large Rectangle.

Make 1

2. Mark 3-5/8" from corner on top left edge of (1) N rectangle. Sew (1) royal F triangle on the top left corner to make a Single Snowball Corner Large Rectangle.

Make 1

Making the Sections

Note: Refer to the diagrams for proper placement and rotation of blocks

Section #1A:

1. Sew (1) medium 3-sided framed block to the top of (1) half snowball square. Make sure the royal A strip and royal F triangles are positioned on the right. Press seam toward the half snowball square. Label the set Left #1A. Make 2.

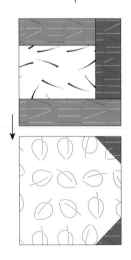
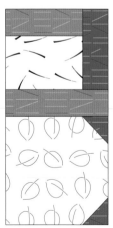

Left #1A
Make 2

2. Sew (1) snowball square to the top of (1) framed square. Make sure the framed square's green strips are positioned at sides. Press seam toward the snowball square. Label the set Right #1A. Make 2.

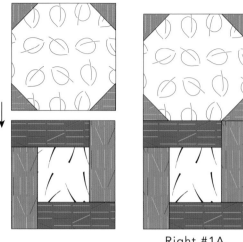

Right #1A
Make 2

3. Sew (1) Left #1A set to (1) Right #1A set aligning tops and matching intersection as shown. Label the sets Section #1A. Make 2.

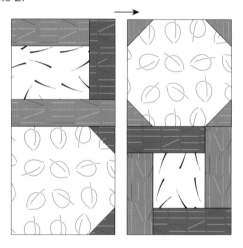

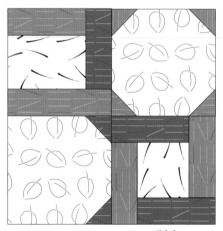

#1A
Make 2

Section #1B:

1. Sew (1) Medium 3-sided Framed Block to the top of (1) Small Single Snowball Corner. Make sure the royal A strip and royal F triangles are positioned on the right. Press seam toward the Small Single Snowball Corner. Label the set Left #1B.

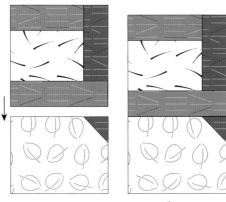

Left #1B

2. Sew (1) Snowball Square to the top of (1) Small 3-sided Framed Block. Make sure the framed block's green strips are positioned at sides. Press seam toward the Snowball Square. Label the set Right #1B.

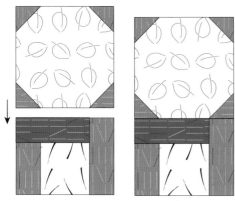

Right #1B

3. Sew (1) Left #1B set to (1) Right #1B set aligning tops and matching intersection as shown. Label as Section #1B.

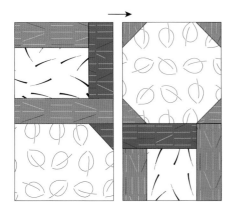

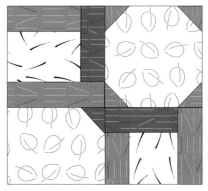

Section #1B

Section #2A:

Sew (1) Large 3-sided Framed Block to the top of (1) Half Snowball Large Rectangle. Make sure the A strip and F triangles meet at left side of block. Label the set Section #2A. Make 2.

Section #2A
Make 2

11

Section #2B:

Sew (1) Large 3-sided Framed Block to the top of (1) Single Snowball Corner Large Rectangle. Make sure the A strip and F triangles meet at left side of block. Label the set Section #2B.

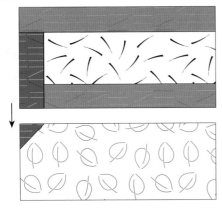

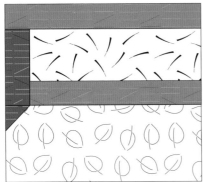

Section #2B

Making the Rows

Row 1 - Sew (1) Small Single Snowball Corner, (1) Small 3-sided Framed Block and (1) Single Snowball Corner Large Rectangle together in a row. Make sure the royal A strip and royal F triangles are positioned on the bottom as shown. Label row 1.

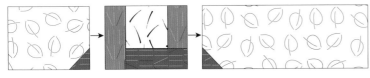

Row 1

Row 2 and 3 - Sew (1) Section#1A to (1) Section #2A aligning tops and matching intersection as shown. Make 2 rows labeling one row 2 and the other row 3.

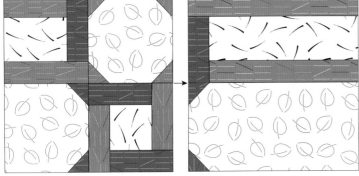

Row 2

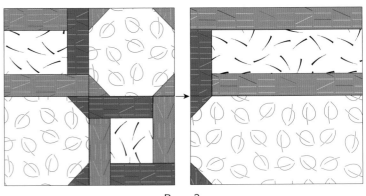

Row 3

Row 4 - Sew (1) Section#1B to (1) Section #2B aligning tops and matching intersection as shown. Label row 4.

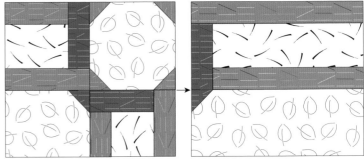

Row 4

Quilt Assembly

1. Referring to the Quilt Center Assembly Diagram, sew the rows together to complete the quilt center.

2. Sew (2) 7-1/2" x WOF royal side border strips together along the short ends. Press the seams open. Sew to the left side of quilt center. Press the seam toward the border and trim even with the quilt center top and bottom. Repeat with the remaining royal 7-1/2" strips and sew to the right side of the quilt center.

3. Sew (2) 2" x WOF royal top and bottom border strips together along the short ends. Press the seams open. Sew to the top of the quilt center. Press the seam toward the border and trim even with quilt center sides. Repeat with the remaining royal 2" strips and sew to the bottom of the quilt center.

Finishing the Quilt

1. Sew the (2) 90" x WOF backing pieces together lengthwise. Press seam open. Layer quilt top, batting and backing together and baste. Tie, hand quilt or machine quilt as desired.

2. Sew the (8) 2-1/4" x WOF strips together into one continuous strip. Press the strip in half lengthwise and sew the binding strip to the raw edge of the quilt top. Fold over raw edges and hand stitch in place on back of quilt.

Quilt Center Assembly Diagram

Ebb & Flow Quilt

Finished quilt size – 60-1/2" x 72"

Yardage

1-1/8 yards white fabric

1-5/8 yards olive fabric

1-1/4 yards dark taupe fabric

5/8 yard yellow-green print fabric

1/2 yard moss print fabric

1/2 yard iris print fabric

1/3 yard gold print fabric

3-3/4 yards backing fabric

68-1/2" x 80" batting

WOF = width of fabric

Cutting

From the white fabric, cut:
(4) 4" x WOF C strips
(2) 3" x WOF D strips

From the olive fabric, cut:
(2) 9-1/2" x 33-1/2" A1 strips
(1) 9-1/2" x 20" A2 strip
(2) 9-1/2" x 26-1/2" A3 strips
(1) 9-1/2" x 13-1/2" A4 strip

From dark taupe fabric, cut:
(8) 3-3/4" x 9-1/2" B1 strips
(4) 5" x WOF strips for side borders
(7) 2-1/4" x WOF strips for binding

From yellow-green print, cut:
(14) 3-3/4" x 9-1/2" B2 strips

From the moss print, cut:
(10) 3-3/4" x 9-1/2" B3 strips

From the iris print fabric, cut:
(12) 3-3/4" x 9-1/2" B4 strips

From gold print fabric, cut:
(6) 3-3/4" x 9-1/2" B5 strips

From the backing fabric, cut:
(2) WOF x 68-1/2" pieces

Sewing Instructions

1. Sew the B strips together along the long edges and in the following order to make a strip set for each row. *Note: To avoid confusion, label each strip section with its coordinating row number.*

Row 1 strip set:

B4   B1   B2   B4   B3   B2

Row 2 strip set:

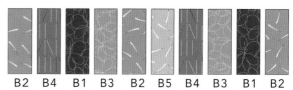

B2   B4   B1   B3   B2   B5   B4   B3   B1   B2

Row 3 strip set:

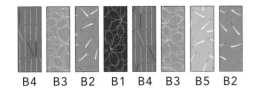

B4   B3   B2   B1   B4   B3   B5   B2

Row 4 strip set:

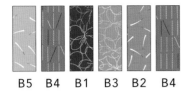

B5   B4   B1   B3   B2   B4

Row 5 strip set:

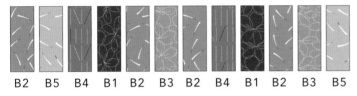

B2 B5 B4 B1 B2 B3 B2 B4 B1 B2 B3 B5

Row 6 strip set:

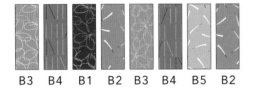

B3   B4   B1   B2   B3   B4   B5   B2

2. Sew the Row strip sets to the A strips in the following order, pressing the seams toward the A strips to complete the quilt rows.

Sew Row 1 strip set to the left side of (1) A1 strip.

Sew Row 2 strip set to the right side of the A2 strip.

Sew Row 3 strip set to the left side of (1) A3 strip.

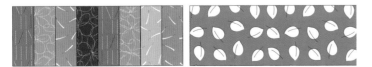

Sew Row 4 strip set to the right side of (1) A1 strip.

Sew Row 5 strip set to the left side of the A4 strip.

Sew Row 6 strip set to the right side of (1) A3 strip.

Quilt Assembly

1. Sew (1) 4" x WOF white C strip to the bottom of rows 1, 2, 4 and 5. Press the seams toward the C strips.

2. Lay out the rows in order beginning with row 1 at the top. Sew the rows together to make the quilt center. Press the seams toward the C strips.

3. Sew the 3" x WOF white D strips to the top and bottom of the quilt center. Press seams toward the D strips.

4. Sew (2) 5" x WOF dark taupe strips together along the short ends. Press. Sew to the left side of quilt center. Press the seam toward the border and trim even with the quilt center top and bottom. Repeat with the remaining dark taupe 5" strips and sew to the right side of the quilt center.

Finishing

1. Sew the (2) WOF x 68-1/2" backing pieces together lengthwise, press seam open. Layer quilt top, batting and backing together and baste. Tie, hand quilt or machine quilt as desired.

2. Sew the (7) 2-1/4" x WOF strips together into one continuous strip. Press the strip in half lengthwise and sew the binding strip to the raw edge of the quilt top. Fold over raw edges and hand stitch in place on back of quilt.

Ebb & Flow Quilt

Finished quilt size – 60-1/2" x 72"

Pieceful Fusion Quilt

Finished quilt size – 64" x 79"
Block sizes—10" x 11" and 12" x 11"

Yardage
2-7/8 yards gray fabric

2-2/3 yards lilac fabric

3/4 yard white fabric

3-3/4 yards backing fabric

72" x 87" batting

WOF = width of fabric

Cutting
From gray fabric, cut:
(12) 1-7/8" x WOF strips
(20) 2-1/8" x WOF strips
(8) 2-1/4" x WOF strips
(4) 3 1/2" x WOF strips

From lilac fabric, cut:
(6) 1-7/8" x WOF strips
(10) 2-1/8" x WOF strips
(11) 2-1/4" x WOF strips; set aside 7 strips for binding
(4) 2" x WOF strips
(4) 6-1/2" x WOF strips

From white fabric, cut:
(3) 1-7/8" x WOF strips
(5) 2-1/8" x WOF strips
(2) 2 1/4" x WOF strips

From backing fabric, cut:
(2) WOF x 72" piece

Sewing Instructions:
1. Sew (1) 1-7/8" x WOF gray strip to either side of (1) 1-7/8" x WOF lilac strip. Press seams toward gray strips to make a gray/lilac/gray strip set. Repeat to make a total of 6 gray/lilac/gray strip sets.

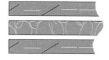

Make 6

2. Sew (1) gray/lilac/gray strip set to either side of (1) 1-7/8" x WOF white strip. Press seams away from white strip. Repeat to make to total of 3 strip sets.

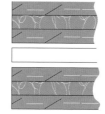

Make 3

3. Subcut the strip sets into (9) 11-1/2" A blocks.

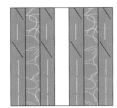

Make 9 A blocks

4. Sew (1) 2-1/8" x WOF gray strip to either side of (1) 2-1/8" x WOF lilac strip. Press seams toward gray strips to make a gray/lilac/gray strip set. Repeat to make a total of 5 gray/lilac/gray strip sets.

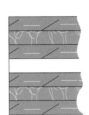

Make 5

5. Sew (1) gray/lilac/gray strip set to either side of (1) 2-1/8" x WOF white strip. Press seams away from white strip. Repeat to make to total of 5 strip sets.

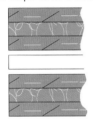

Make 5

6. Subcut 3 of the strip sets into (9) 10-1/2" B blocks and 2 of the strip sets into (6) 12-1/2" C blocks.

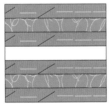

Make 9 B blocks   Make 6 C blocks

7. Sew (1) 2-1/4" x WOF gray strip to either side of (1) 2-1/4" x WOF lilac strip. Press seams toward gray strips to make a gray/lilac/gray strip set. Repeat to make a total of 2 gray/lilac/gray strip sets.

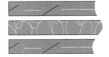

Make 2

8. Sew (1) gray/lilac/gray strip set to either side of (1) 2-1/4" x WOF white strip. Press seams away from white strip. Repeat to make to total of 2 strip sets.

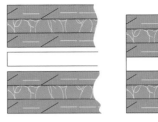

Make 2

9. Subcut the strip sets into (6) 11-1/2" D blocks

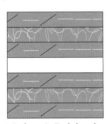

Make 6 D blocks

Quilt Assembly

1. Lay out the blocks in **vertical rows,** alternating the blocks as shown in the Quilt Assembly Diagram.

Note: Rows 1, 3 and 5 start with Block A and alternate with Block B. Rows 2 and 4 start with Block C and alternate with Block D.

2. Sew the blocks together in vertical rows. Press the seams in the odd-numbered rows down and the seams in the even-numbered rows up.

3. Lay out the rows in order, beginning with row 1 on the left. Sew the vertical rows together two at a time. Sew the sets of rows together to make the quilt center.

4. Sew (2) 3-1/2" x WOF gray strips together along the short ends. Press. Sew to the left side of the quilt center. Press the seam toward the border and trim even with the quilt center top and bottom. Repeat with the remaining gray 3-1/2" strips and sew to the right side of the quilt center.

5. Sew (2) 2" x WOF lilac strips together along the short ends. Press. Sew to the left side of the quilt center. Press the seam toward the border and trim even with the quilt center top and bottom. Repeat with the remaining lilac 2" strips and sew to the right side of the quilt center.

6. Sew (2) 6 1/2" x WOF lilac strips together along the short ends. Press. Sew to the top of the quilt center. Press the seam toward the border and trim even with the quilt center sides. Repeat with the remaining lilac 6-1/2" strips and sew to the bottom to complete the quilt top.

Finishing the Quilt

1. Sew the (2) WOF x 72" backing pieces together lengthwise. Press seam open. Layer quilt top, batting and backing together and baste. Tie, hand quilt or machine quilt as desired.

2. Sew the (7) 2-1/4 " x WOF strips together into one continuous strip. Press the strip in half lengthwise and sew the binding strip to the raw edge of the quilt top. Fold over raw edges and hand stitch in place on back of quilt.

Quilt Assembly Diagram

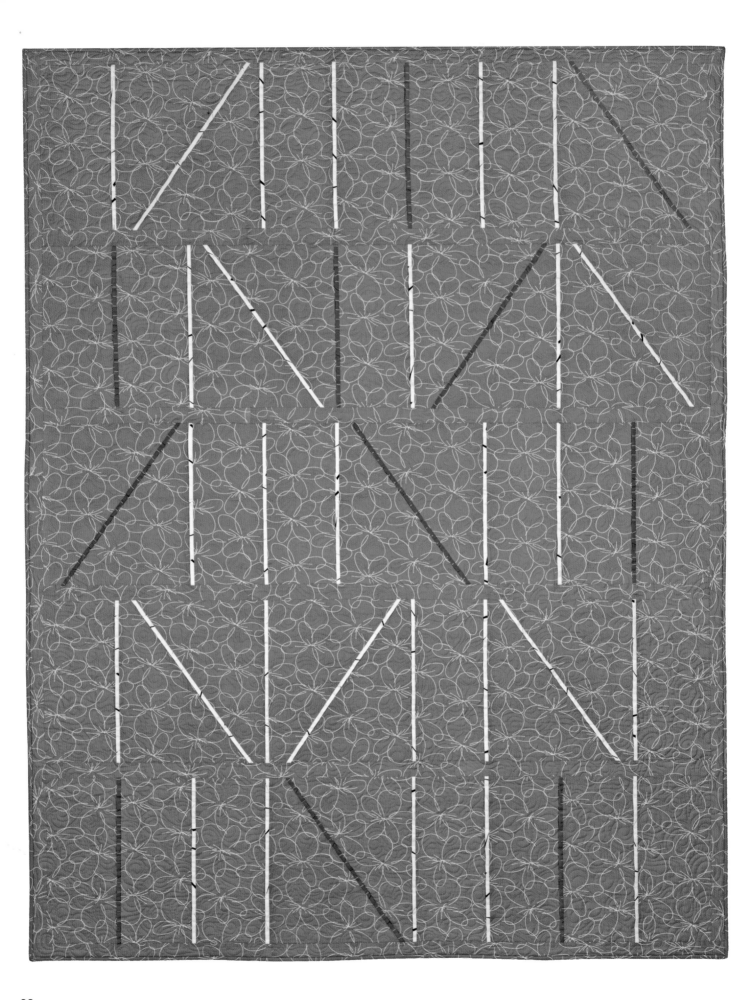

Pick Up Sticks Quilt

Finished quilt size – 66" x 84"

Yardage

5-1/4 yards moss print fabric

3/4 yard white fabric

3/4 yard iris fabric

5 yards backing fabric

72" x 90" batting

WOF = width of fabric

Cutting

Note: Lightly starch this fabric BEFORE cutting.

From the moss print fabric, cut:
(23) 7-1/2" x 15-1/2" pieces
(6) 2" x WOF sashing strips
(8) 1-3/4" x WOF border strips
(8) 2-1/4" x WOF binding strips
(11) 15-1/4" x 15-1/2" rectangles

From the white fabric, cut:
(6) 1-1/4" x 19-1/2" strips
(23) 1-1/4" x 15-1/2" strips

From the iris fabric, cut:
(5) 1-1/4" x 19-1/2" strips
(6) 1-1/4" x 15-1/2" strips

From the backing fabric, cut:
(2) 90" x WOF pieces

Sewing Instructions

Making the Angled Blocks

1. Measure and mark 2" in from the top left corner of a 15-1/4" x 15-1/2" moss rectangle. Measure and mark 2" in from the bottom right corner of the rectangle. Draw a diagonal line between the top and bottom marks. Cut along the marked line to make a left and right section.

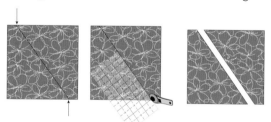

2. Fold a 1-1/4" x 19-1/2" iris strip in half lengthwise, wrong sides together, and press. Place the folded strip on the angled edge of the left section, matching the raw edges. Baste the pieces together using a scant 1/4" seam.

3. Layer the left section on top of the right section, matching the angled edges. Using a 1/4" seam, sew through all the layers to make an AC Left block (ACL). Press the block so the folded strip lies flat with the fold facing down. The block should measure 14-1/2" x 15-1/2". Make a total of 3 ACL blocks.

Make 3
ACL blocks

4. Following steps 1-3 use (4) 15-1/4" x 15-1/2" moss rectangles and (4) 1-1/4" x 19-1/2" white strips to make 4 ABL blocks.

Make 4
ABL blocks

5. Measure and mark 2" in from the top right corner of a 15-1/4" x 15-1/2" moss rectangle. Measure and mark 2" in from the bottom left corner of the rectangle. Draw a diagonal line between the top and bottom marks. Cut along the marked line to make a left and right section.

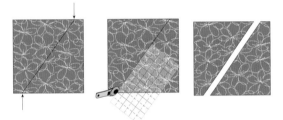

6. Fold a 1-1/4" x 19-1/2" iris strip in half lengthwise, wrong sides together, and press. Place the folded strip on the angled edge of the right section, matching the raw edges. Baste the pieces together using a scant 1/4" seam.

7. Layer the right section on top of the left section, matching the angled edges. Using a 1/4" seam, sew through all the layers to make an AC Right block (ACR). Press the block so the folded strip lies flat with the fold facing down. The block should measure 14-1/2" x 15-1/2". Make a total of 2 ACR blocks.

Make 2
ACR blocks

8. Following steps 6-8 use (2) 15-1/4" x 15-1/2" moss rectangles and (2) 1-1/4" x 19-1/2" white strips to make 2 ABR blocks.

Make 2
ABR blocks

24

Making the Strip Blocks

1. Press a 1-1/4" x 15-1/2" white strip, wrong sides together, in half lengthwise. Lay the folded strip on the right edge of a 7-1/2" x 15-1/2" moss piece, matching the raw edges. Baste in place using a scant 1/4" seam to make an AB set. Repeat to make 15 AB sets.

2. Following step 1 use (5) 7-1/2" x 15-1/2" moss pieces and (5) 1-1/4" x 15-1/2" iris strips to make 5 AC sets.

3. Press the remaining 1-1/4" x 15-1/2" white and iris strips, in half lengthwise with wrong sides together.

4. Sew a folded white strip to the right side of each of the following blocks (2) ABR, (2) ACR, (2) ACL and (2) ABL to make 2 ABR-B, 2 ACR-B, 2 ACL-B and 2 ABL-B blocks.

5. Sew a folded iris strip to the right side of an ABL block to make an ABL-C block.

Quilt Assembly

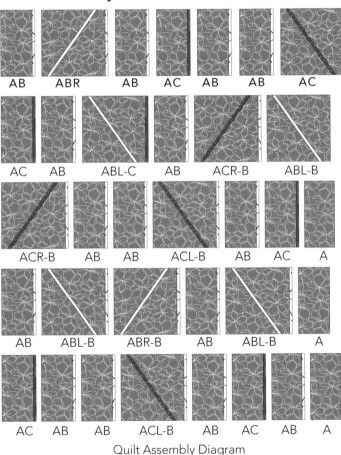

Quilt Assembly Diagram

1. Referring to the Quilt Assembly Diagram, lay out the blocks and 7-1/2" x 15-1/2" moss A pieces in 5 horizontal rows.

Row 1 – AB, ABR, AB, AC, AB, AB, ACL
Row 2 – AC, AB, ABL-C, AB, ACR-B, ABL-B
Row 3 – ACR-B, AB, AB, ACL-B, AB, AC, A
Row 4 – AB, ABL-B, ABR-B, AB, ABL-B, A
Row 5 – AC, AB, AB, ACL-B, AB, AC, AB, A

2. Sew the blocks together in rows.

3. Sew (2) 2" x WOF moss sashing strips together along the short edges to make 1 strip. Sew the strip to the bottom of Row 1. Press the seam toward the strip. Trim any excess fabric from the strip and set aside.

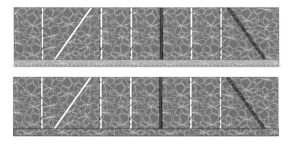

4. Following step 3, sew sashing strips to the bottom of rows 2 and 3. Sew the extra strips trimmed from each sashing together to make the sashing strip for row 4.

5. Lay out the rows in order with row 1 at the top and row 5 at the bottom. With a marking pencil, extend the seam line of the AB and AC blocks through the sashing to aid in matching the folded strips within each row.

6. Sew rows 1 and 2 together, matching the seams to the marks on the sashing.

Row 1

Row 2

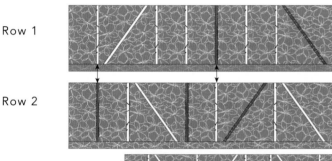

In the same manner, sew row 4 to row 5. Sew row 3 to the bottom of row 2. Sew the bottom of row 3 to the top of row 4. Press the seams in the same direction to complete the quilt center.

Row 3

Row 4

Row 5

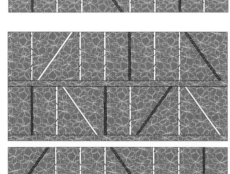

7. Sew (2) 1-3/4" x WOF moss border strips together along the short edges to make 1 strip. Press. Sew the strip to the left side of quilt center. Press and trim the strip even with the quilt center top and bottom. In the same manner, sew a border to the right side of the quilt center. Press and trim.

8. Sew (2) 1-3/4" x WOF moss border strips together along the short edges to make 1 strip. Press. Sew to the top of the quilt center. Press and trim even with the quilt sides. In the same manner, sew a border to the bottom of the quilt center. Press and trim

Finishing

1. Sew the (2) 90" x WOF backing pieces together lengthwise. Press seam open. Layer quilt top, batting and backing together and baste. Tie, hand quilt or machine quilt as desired.

2. Sew the (8) 2-1/4" x WOF strips together into one continuous strip. Press the strip in half lengthwise, wrong sides together, and sew to the raw edge of the quilt top. Fold over raw edges and hand stitch in place on back of quilt.

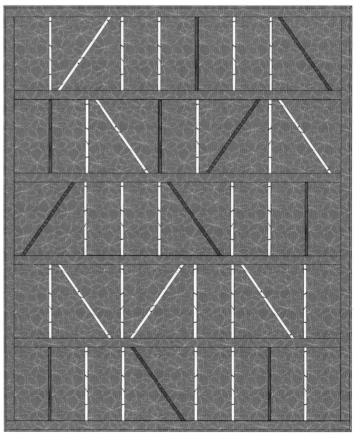

Yoga Mat

Finished size – 25" x 57"

Yardage

Fat eighth (9" x 22")
black on white fabric

1/3 yard grass green fabric

1/3 yard royal fabric

1-1/4 yards aqua fabric

1/2 yard blue fabric

Fat eighth (9" x 22") white print fabric

Fat eighth (9" x 22")
white leaf print fabric

Fat eighth (9" x 22") white fabric

Fat eighth (9" x 22") teal fabric

1-3/4 yards backing fabric

31" x 63" batting

31" x 63" non-stick mesh

WOF = width of fabric

Cutting

From the grass green fabric, cut:
(1) 8-1/2" x 24" B piece
(1) 8-1/2" x 13-1/2" E piece

From the royal fabric, cut:
(1) 8-1/2" x 24" B piece
(1) 8-1/2" x 13-1/2" E piece

From the aqua fabric, cut:
(1) 4-1/2" x 9-5/8" C piece
(1) 4-1/2" x 18-7/8" D piece
(1) 3-1/2" H square
(5) 1-1/2" x WOF border strips
(5) 2-1/4" x WOF binding strips

From the blue fabric, cut:
(1) 4-1/2" x 18-7/8" D piece
(1) 4-1/2" x 9-5/8" C piece
(2) 3-1/2" x 26-1/2" G pieces

From the white print fat eighth, cut:
(1) 8-1/2" F square

From the white leaf print fat eighth, cut:
(1) 8-1/2" F square

From the white fat eighth, cut:
(1) 8-1/2" F square

From the teal fat eighth, cut:
(1) 8-1/2" x 13-1/2" E piece

From the backing fabric, cut:
(1) 31" x 63" piece

Sewing Instructions

Mat Assembly

1. Referring to the Mat Assembly Diagram, lay out the pieces in 4 rows as shown. Sew the pieces together in rows.

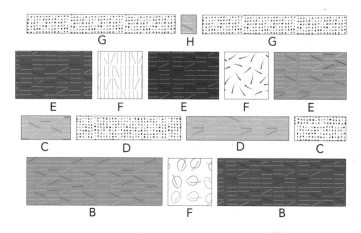

Note: Mark the center of each row, matching the centers of the rows before sewing them together. This will make it easier to evenly distribute the rows.

2. Sew row 1 to row 2 and row 3 to row 4. Sew the pairs of rows together to make the mat center.

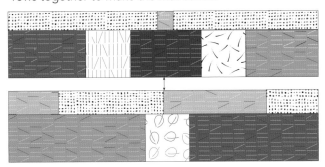

3. Sew (2) 1-1/2" x WOF aqua border strips together along the short edges to make 1 strip. Press the seam open. Sew the strip to one long side of the mat center. Press the seam toward the border. Trim the strip even with the short edges of the mat. In the same manner, sew a border to the other long side of the mat center. Press and trim.

4. Sew a 1-1/2" x WOF aqua border strip to opposite short edges of the mat center. Press and trim the borders even with the sides.

Finishing the Mat

1. Layer the mat top, batting and backing together and baste. Tie, hand quilt or machine quilt as desired.

Note: If you are making the yoga mat, place the non-stick mesh on the right side of the backing and tack in several places. Our long arm quilter placed the non-stick mesh on the backing before she quilted. If machine quilting on a home machine, the mesh will not go through feed dogs smoothly, so it should be added AFTER quilting is done.

2. Sew the (5) 2-1/4" x WOF aqua binding strips together into one continuous strip. Press the strip in half lengthwise, wrong sides together, and sew to the raw edge of the mat top. Fold over raw edges and hand stitch in place on the back of the mat.

Color Option

Zen Garden Quilt

Finished size – 62" x 82"
Block size – 10" square

Yardage

1-1/4 yards dark taupe fabric
1-1/4 yards white on gray fabric
1-1/4 yards gray fabric
1-1/4 yards gray on white fabric
1/2 yard white print fabric
1 yard royal fabric
1 yard iris fabric
1 yard grass green fabric
1 yard light fuchsia fabric
5 yards backing fabric
68" x 90" batting

WOF = width of fabric

Cutting

Note: We highly recommend that you starch the fabrics before cutting the templates.

From dark taupe fabric, cut: (12) template A on page 34

From white on gray fabric, cut: (12) template C on page 35

From gray fabric, cut: (12) template G on page 35

From gray on white fabric, cut: (12) template E on page 34

From white print fabric, cut: (8) 2-1/4" x WOF strips for binding

From royal fabric, cut: (12) template B on page 36

From iris fabric, cut: (12) template D on page 37

From grass green fabric, cut:
(7) 2" x WOF strips for border
(12) template H on page 37

From light fuchsia fabric, cut: (12) template F on page 36

From backing fabric, cut: (2) 90" x WOF pieces

Sewing Instructions

1. Match the center curve marks and the edges of the curves, pinning in place. Using a 1/4" seam, ease the A curve to the B curve as the pieces are sewn together. Only clip the edge of the A curve when necessary to ease the pieces together smoothly. Press seam toward A to make a Drunkard's Path square.

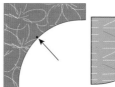

2. Referring to step 1 make the following combinations of Drunkard's Path squares: (12) AB squares, (12) DC squares, (12) EF squares and (12) GH squares.

Quilt Assembly

1. Referring to the Quilt Assembly Diagram, lay out the Drunkard's Path squares in 8 rows with 6 squares in each row. Carefully follow the diagram for the correct rotation of each square.

Quilt Assembly Diagram

2. Sew the squares together in pairs. Sew pairs from rows 1 and 2 together to make 3 circle blocks. Repeat this process for rows 3 and 4, rows 5 and 6 and rows 7 and 8 to make a total of 12 circle blocks.

3. Press the seams in each row in the same direction.

4. Sew the rows together to make the quilt center. Press the seams in the same direction.

5. Sew (2) 2" x WOF grass green border strips together along the short edges to make 1 strip. Press. Sew the strip to the left side of quilt center. Press toward border strip and trim even with the quilt center top and bottom. In the same manner, sew a border to the right side of the quilt center. Press and trim.

6. Sew (2) 2" x WOF grass green border strips together along the short edges to make 1 strip. Press. Sew to the top of the quilt center. Press toward the border and trim even with the quilt sides. In the same manner, sew the trimmed border strip and a 2" x WOF grass green border strip together along the short edges to make 1 strip. Press. Sew to the bottom of the quilt center. Press toward border and trim.

Finishing

1. Sew the (2) 90" x WOF backing pieces together lengthwise, press seam open. Layer quilt top, batting and backing together and baste. Tie, hand quilt or machine quilt as desired.

2. Sew the (8) 2-1/4" x WOF strips together into one continuous strip. Press the strip in half lengthwise, wrong sides together, and sew to the raw edge of the quilt top. Fold over raw edges and hand stitch in place on back of quilt.

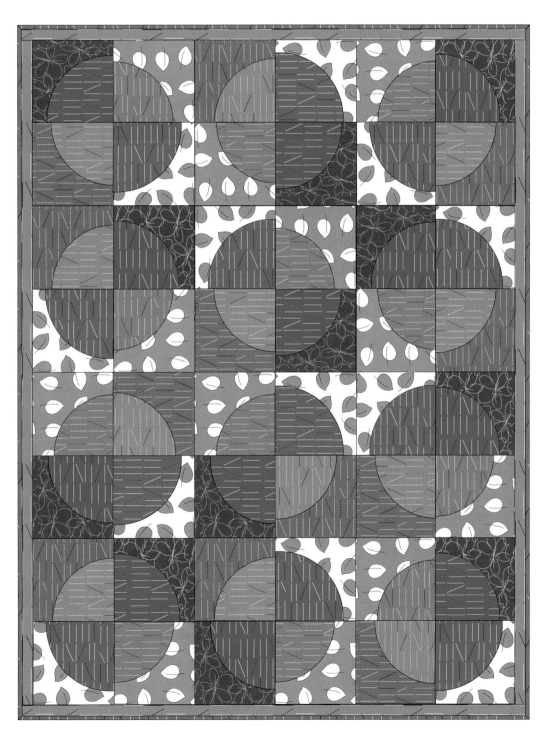

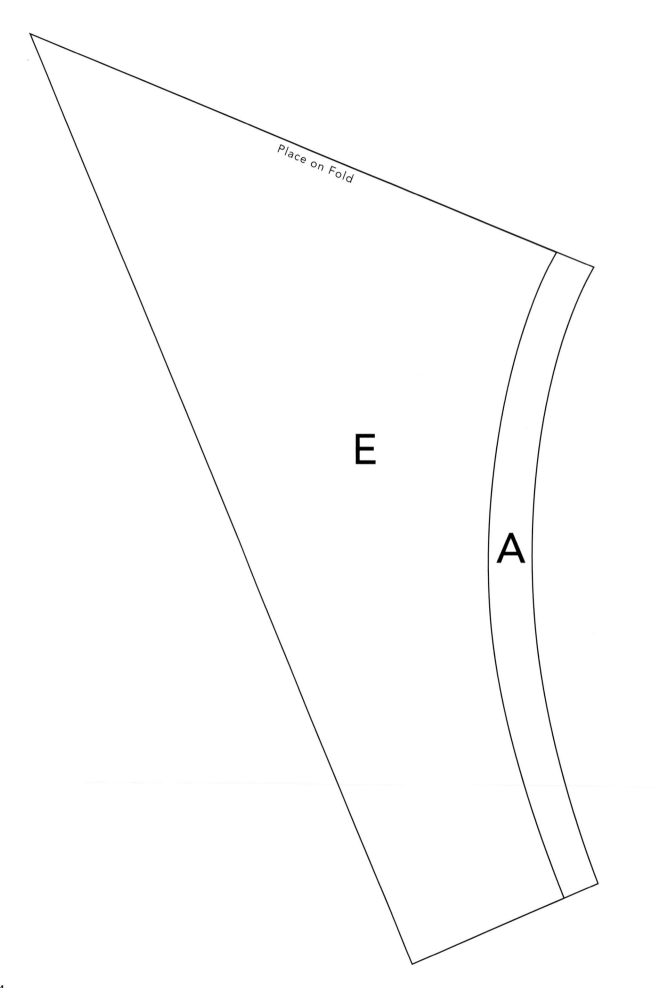

Place on Fold

E

A

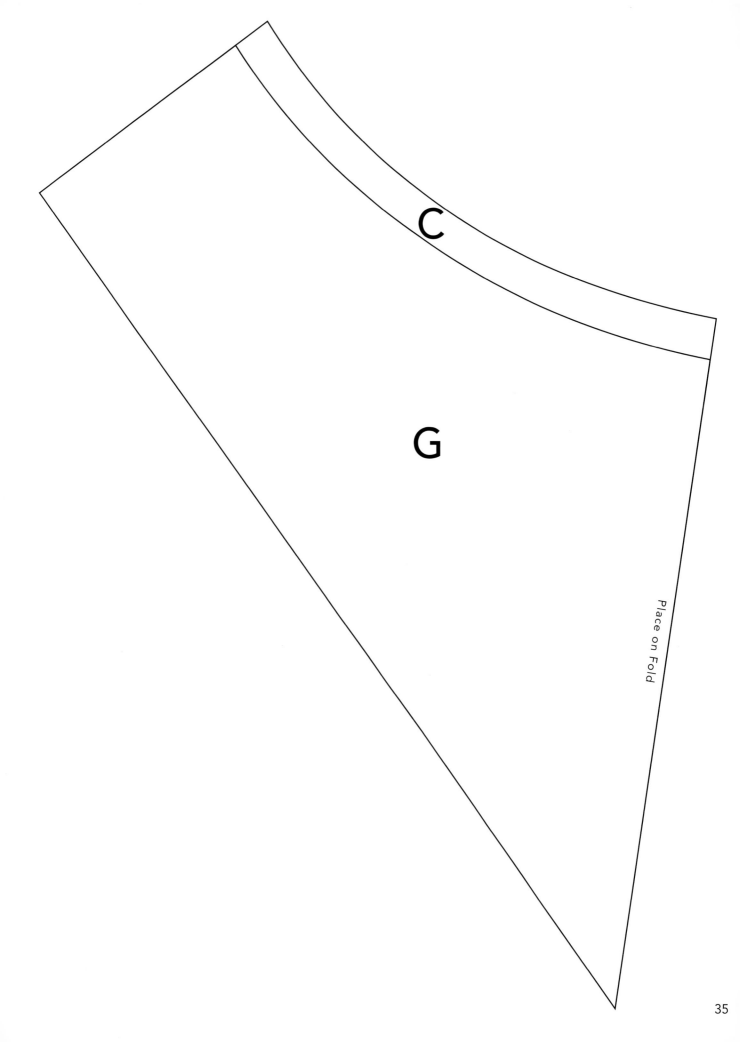

C

G

Place on Fold

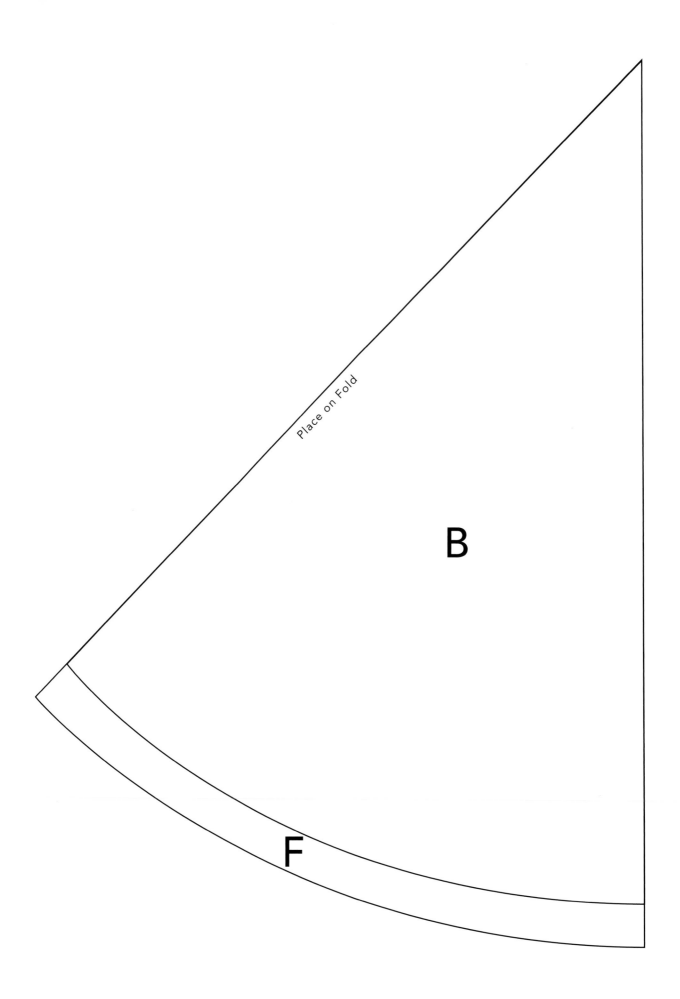

Place on Fold

B

F

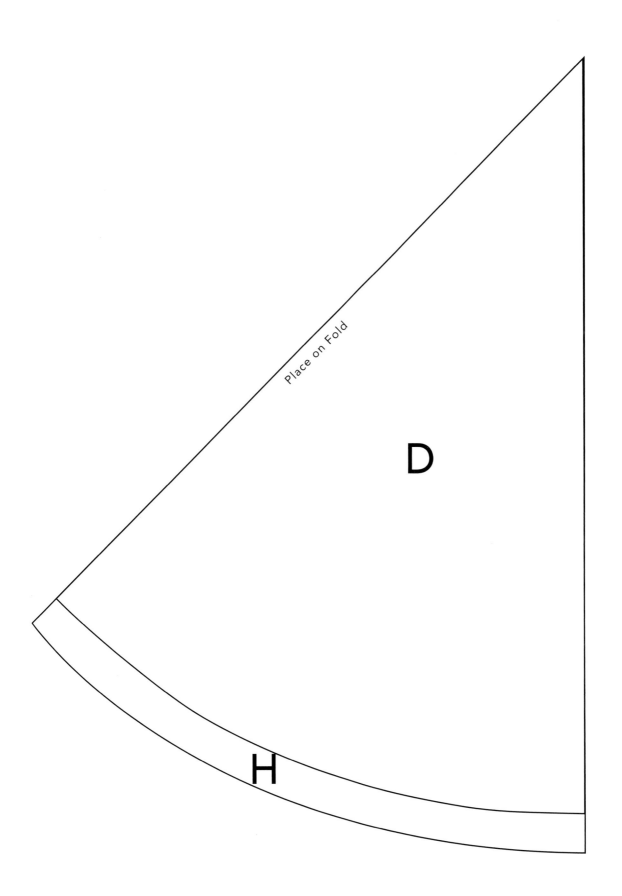

Place on Fold

D

H

Cherry Blossom Quilt

Finished size – 67" x 93"

Yardage

1-3/8 yards white fabric
1-3/4 yards white print fabric
1-1/8 yards black flower on white fabric
1-1/4 yards black-on-white print fabric
2-1/8 yards fuchsia fabric
5-3/4 yards backing fabric
75" x 103" batting

Cutting

From white fabric, cut:
(2) 11" squares; sub cut twice on the diagonal to make
8 quarter-square triangles
(1) 10-1/4" x 15" piece
(1) 10-1/4" x 12-1/2" piece
(1) 10-1/4" x 29-3/4" piece
(2) 8-1/2" x WOF strips. Sew the strips together and cut:
(1) 8-1/2" x 59-1/2" piece
and (1) 8-1/2" x 22-1/2" piece

From the white print fabric, cut:
(2) 11" squares; sub cut twice on the diagonal to make
8 quarter-square triangles
(1) 30" x 8-1/2" piece (cut along length of fabric)
(1) 35-3/4" x 6-1/2" piece (cut along length of fabric)
(3) 3-1/2" x WOF strips. Sew the strips together and cut:
(1) 3-1/2" x 88-1/2" strip
(3) 5-1/2" x WOF strips. Sew the strips together and cut:
(1) 5-1/2" x 88-1/2" strip

From the black flower on white fabric, cut:
(2) 11" squares; sub cut twice on the diagonal to make
8 quarter-square triangles
(1) 10-1/4" x 42" piece
(1) 10-1/4" x 39-1/2" piece
(2) 8-1/2" x WOF strips. Sew the strips together and cut:
(1) 8-1/2" x 66-1/2" strip. Cut the remaining piece of the strip to
4-1/2" wide.
(2) 4-1/2" x WOF strips. Sew the strips and remaining 4-1/2" strip together
along the short ends and cut: (1) 4-1/2" x 88 1/2" strip

From the black-on-white print fabric, cut:
(2) 11" squares; sub cut twice on the diagonal to make
8 quarter-square triangles
(1) 10-1/4" x 39-1/2" piece
(2) 10-1/4" x 20" pieces
(2) 6-1/2" x WOF strips. Sew the strips together and cut:
(1) 6-1/2" x 53-3/8" strip

From the fuchsia fabric, cut:
(5) 2" x WOF strips. Sew the strips together and cut: (2) 2" x 88-1/2" strips
(4) 2-3/4" x WOF strips
(8) 2-1/4" x WOF binding strips
(24) 1-1/2" x WOF strips

From the backing fabric, cut:
(2) 103" x WOF pieces

Sewing Instructions

1. Sew a white quarter-square triangle and a white print quarter-square triangle together as shown. Press the seam toward the white triangle to make an AB triangle set. Make a total of 2 AB triangle sets. In the same manner, make 2 BA triangle sets.

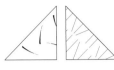  

Make 2 AB triangle sets   Make 2 BA triangle sets

2. Sew a black flower on white quarter-square triangle to a black-on-white quarter-square triangle as shown. Press the seam toward the black flower on white triangle to make a CD triangle set. Make a total of 2 CD triangle sets.

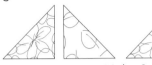

Make 2 CD triangle sets

3. Sew a black-on-white quarter-square triangle to a black flower on white quarter-square triangle. Press the seam toward the black-on-white triangle to make a DC triangle set. Make a total of 2 DC triangle sets.

Make 2 DC triangle sets

4. Sew a black flower on white quarter-square triangle to a white quarter-square triangle. Press the seam toward the black flower on white triangle to make 1 CA triangle set.

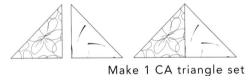

Make 1 CA triangle set

5. Sew black-on-white quarter-square triangle to a white print quarter-square triangle. Press the seam toward the black-on-white triangle to make 1 DB triangle set.

Make 1 DB triangle set

6. Sew an AB triangle set to a CD triangle set as shown. Press the seam open to make 1 Quad 1.

Make 1 Quad 1

7. Sew a BA triangle set to a DC triangle set as shown. Press the seam open to make 1 Quad 1B.

Make 1 Quad 1B

8. Sew a CA triangle set to a DB triangle set. Press the seam open to make 1 Quad 5.

Make 1 Quad 5

9. Sew an AB triangle set to a DC triangle set. Press the seam open to make 1 Quad 9.

Make 1 Quad 9

10. .Sew a BA triangle set to a CD triangle set. Press the seam open to make 1 Quad 9B.

Make 1 Quad 9B

11. Square all the Quad sets to 10-1/2".

Quilt Assembly

1. Referring to the Quilt Assembly Diagram, lay out the pieces and Quad sets in vertical rows as shown. Carefully watch the orientation of the Quad sets; the triangles should match the fabric print on all sides. Sew the pieces in each vertical row together in order, beginning with the top piece.

Vertical row 1:
(1) 10-1/4 x 15" white piece, (1) Quad 1,
(1) 10-1/4" x 42" black flower on white piece,
(1) Quad 1B, (1) 10-1/4 x 12-1/2" white piece

Vertical row 2:
(1) 2" x 88-1/2" fuchsia strip

Vertical row 3:
(1) 5-1/2" x 88-1/2" white print strip

Vertical row 4:
(1) 8-1/2" x 59-1/2" white piece,
(1) 8-1/2" x 30" white print piece

Vertical row 5:
(1) 10-1/4" x 39-1/2" black-on-white print piece, (1) Quad 5,
(1) 10-1/4" x 39-1/2" black flower on white piece

Vertical row 6:
(1) 3-1/2" x 88-1/2" white print strip

Vertical row 7:
(1) 8-1/2" x 66-1/2" black flower on white piece,
(1) 8-1/2" x 22-1/2" white piece

Vertical row 8:
    (1) 6-1/2" x 35-3/4" white print piece,
    (1) 6-1/2" x 53-3/8" black-on-white print strip

Vertical row 9:
    (1) 10-1/4 x 20" black-on-white print piece,
    (1) Quad 9, (1) 10-1/4" x 29-3/4" white piece, (1)
    Quad 9B, 10-1/4" x 20" black-on-white print piece

Vertical row 10:
    (1) 2" x 88-1/2" fuchsia strip

Vertical row 11:
    (1) 4-1/2" x 88-1/2" black flower on white strip

2.   Sew the vertical rows together in pairs. Sew the pairs together to finish the quilt top.

3.   Sew (2) 2-3/4" x WOF fuchsia strips together along the short ends. Press the seam open. Sew to the top of the quilt center. Press the seam toward the border and trim even with the quilt sides. Repeat with the remaining 2-3/4" fuchsia strips and sew to the bottom of the quilt center. Press and trim.

Finishing

1.   Sew the (2) 103" x WOF backing pieces together lengthwise. Press the seam open. Layer quilt top, batting and backing together and baste. Tie, hand quilt or machine quilt as desired.

2.   Sew the (8) 2-1/4" x WOF binding strips together into one continuous strip. Press the strip in half lengthwise and sew the binding strip to the raw edge of the quilt top. Fold over raw edges and hand stitch in place on back of quilt.

Adding the Flowers

1.   Sew (3) 1-1/2" x WOF fuchsia strips together along the short ends to make a continuous strip. Repeat to make a total of 8 continuous strips.

2.   Fold a continuous strip in thirds lengthwise and with wrong sides together. One of the long edges should slightly overlap the other. Press. Repeat with the remaining continuous strips.

3.   Using a strong quilting weight thread, sew a gathering stitch down the center of the strips through all layers. Slightly gather each strip and pin on the quilt top in big curves to form flower shapes. Note: We used 2 strips per flower. Enlarge the flower motif from the black flower on white fabric for reference to make the flower whatever size you wish.

4.   Hand or machine stitch through center of gathered strip to complete the flowers.

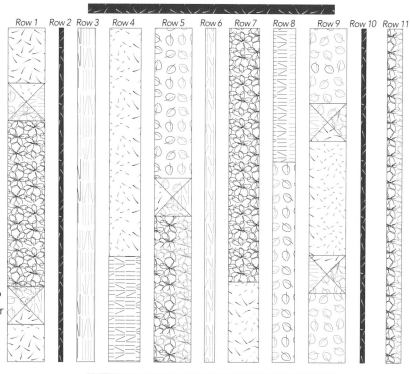

Quilt Assembly Diagram

41

Yukata Robe

Sizes: Small/Medium and Large/Extra-Large

Yardage

3 yards claret red fabric

Cutting

From claret red fabric, cut:

	Small/Medium	Large/Extra-large
Front	(2) 17" x WOF pieces	(2) 19" x WOF pieces
Back	(1) 25" x WOF piece	(1) 27" x WOF piece
Sleeve	(2) 14" x 23-3/4" pieces	(2) 14" x 25-1/2" pieces
Neckband	(2) 4-3/4" x WOF strips	(2) 4-3/4" x WOF strips
Ties	(4) 1-1/2" x 15" strips	(4) 1-1/2" x 15" strips

WOF = width of fabric
Sew with a 1/2" seam allowance

Sewing Instructions

Yukata Front and Back

1. Trim the selvage off one end of each 17" x WOF front piece. MARK the trimmed end as the top of the front pieces.

2. Place the front pieces wrong sides together, matching the selvage and raw edges. Measure 9-1/2" in from the upper right corner on the top edge and mark. Beginning in the upper left corner, measure 25" down the left side and mark.

3. Using a long ruler draw a line from the top mark to the side mark. Cut on the line through both front pieces. This creates the center angle for the yukata front.

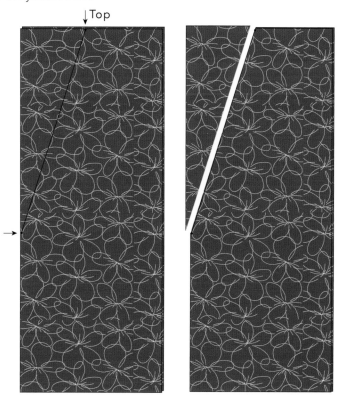

4. Trim the selvage off one end of the 25" x WOF back piece. MARK the trimmed end as the top of the back piece. Find the center of the back piece on the top edge and mark.

5. Place the back piece and front pieces right sides together, matching the top corners and sides. Pin in place. Sew all the way across the back piece to create shoulder seams. Press the seam allowance open.

6. Zigzag stitch the edge of the seam allowances.

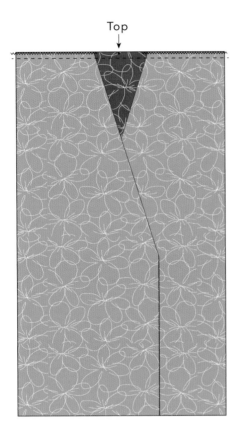

Top

Sleeves

1. Fold each of the 14" x 23-3/4" sleeve pieces in half lengthwise and mark the middle of each piece.

2. On the long edge of each sleeve create a double-fold 1/2" hem. Stitch close to the folded edge.

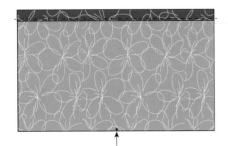

3. Place the long raw edge of the sleeve on one side of the robe, right sides together. Match up the middle mark with the shoulder seam on the sleeve piece. Sew in place.

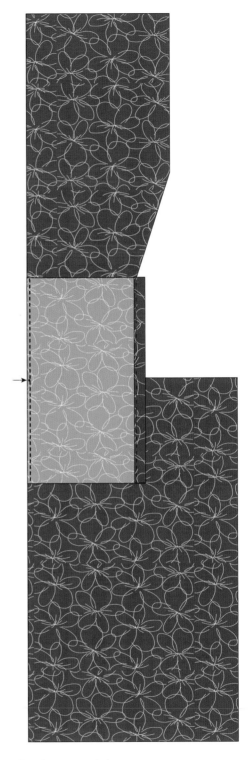

4. Repeat for the second sleeve.

Ties

Fold a 1-1/2" x 15" strip in half lengthwise. Sew 1/4" seam along one short end and side of strip. Turn the strip right side out and press. Topstitch to complete a tie. Repeat with the remaining (3) 1-1/2" x 15" strips to make a total of 4 ties.

Yukata Assembly

1. Measure 5" down from the left armpit corner of the robe and mark. On the right side of the fabric, place the raw edge of a tie on the left front side edge of the robe and baste in place. Pin the loose end of the tie to the bodice to avoid getting it caught when sewing the side seam.

2. Place the raw edge of another tie 5" down from the right armpit of the robe on the wrong side of the fabric and baste in place. Pin the loose end of the tie to the bodice to avoid getting it caught when sewing the side seam.

3. Measure 10" up from the bottom edge on the front and back side seams and mark. With right sides together, sew side seams beginning at the hemmed sleeve edge, pivoting at robe/sleeve corner and continuing down side of robe body to the 10" mark. Trim the sleeve/body corner. Zigzag stitch the edge of the seam allowances.

4. Double-fold 1/4" along each remaining unsewn side seam. Stitch close to the fold and sew to bottom edge of robe.

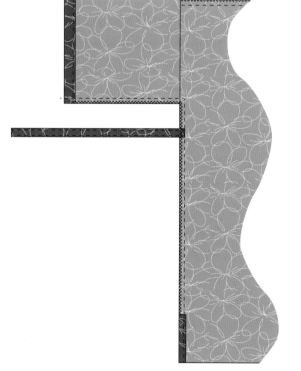

5. Double fold 1/4" along one front inside edge of the robe, just below angled edge. Stitch close to the fold. Repeat on remaining front piece.

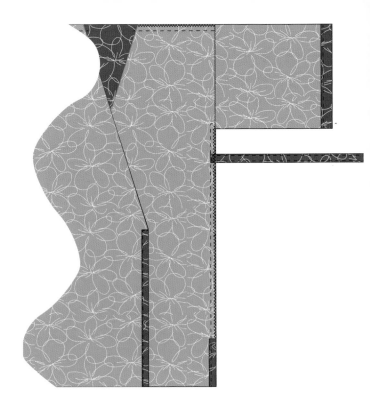

6. To make the neckband sew the 4-3/4" x WOF strips together along one short end. Measure the angled edges of the robe's neckline and trim the strip to this measurement. It should measure approximately 59".

7. Fold in one long edge of the strip 1/4" to the wrong side of the fabric and press. Fold in the short ends 1/2" and press.

8. Fold neckband piece in half lengthwise and mark the middle.

9. With right sides together, place the neckband's raw edge on the angled edge of the robe's neckline matching the center mark on back piece. The folded neckband ends should be approximately 1/4" past the bottom of each angled edge. Sew in place. Clip seam allowance at shoulder seams and neck. Press seam toward neckband.

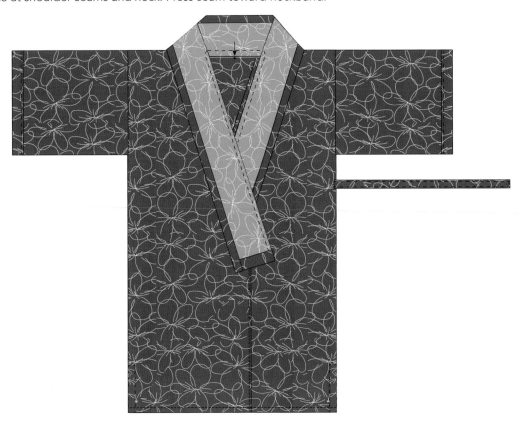

10. Measure 5" up from end of neckband and mark. Place the raw edge of one tie on the robe side of the seam allowance and baste in place. Make sure the tie lays to the robe side not neckband side. Pin the tie in place so it doesn't get caught in the finishing seam. Repeat on other side of neckband.

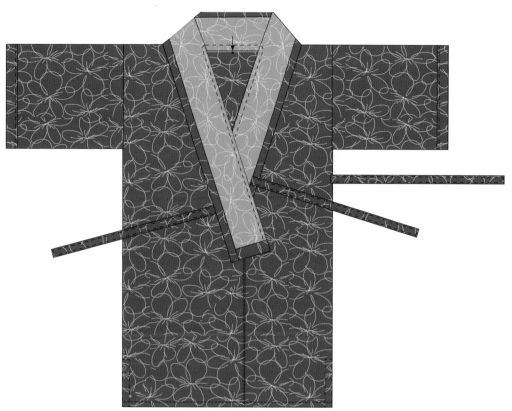

11. Fold the neckband in half, wrong sides together, and pin it even with the seam just sewn. With right side of robe facing up, sew close to the seam edge on the neckband.

12. Tack the tie in place against inside edge of neckband.

13. Make a 1/2" double-fold along the bottom of robe and sew close to the folded edge to hem the robe.

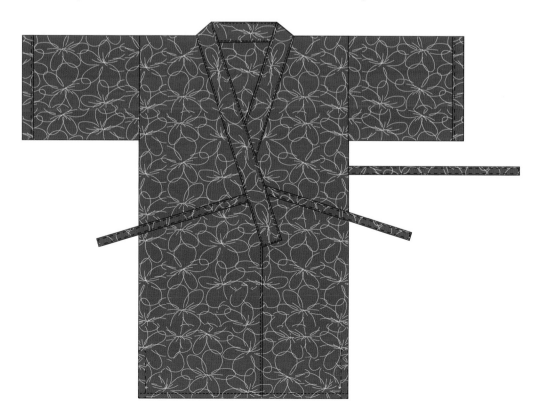

Relaxation Mask

Yardage

Fat eighth gold print fabric

1/2 yard of 3/4" or 1" gross grain
ribbon or twill tape

18" of 1/4" wide elastic

Flax seed (we use flax seed as it is
smaller and forms to your eye better)

Cutting

From gold print fabric, cut:
(2) eye mask templates on page 49

Sewing Instructions

1. Fold the ribbon or twill tape in half lengthwise. Sew close to the edge to make a casing. Using a safety pin, pull the elastic through the casing and secure at one end. As you pull through stretch the elastic to create the tightness you desire. Secure the remaining end and trim any excess.

2. Position the elastic ribbon across the right side of 1 mask piece, aligning the raw ends at marks on each side of mask piece. Baste in place. Place the remaining mask piece on top, right sides together, with ribbon sandwiched between the pieces. Begin sewing the pieces together at the top, slightly off center and continue sewing, leaving a 1 – 1-1/2" opening at top.

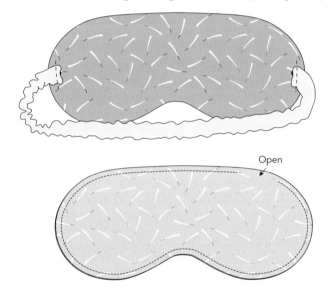

Open

3. Turn the pieces right side out and press. Fill the eye mask with flax seed to the desired thickness. Stitch the top opening closed, continuing the stitching around the eye mask close to the edge. Top stitch another seam 1/4" from the edge all the way around the mask.

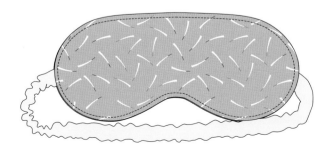

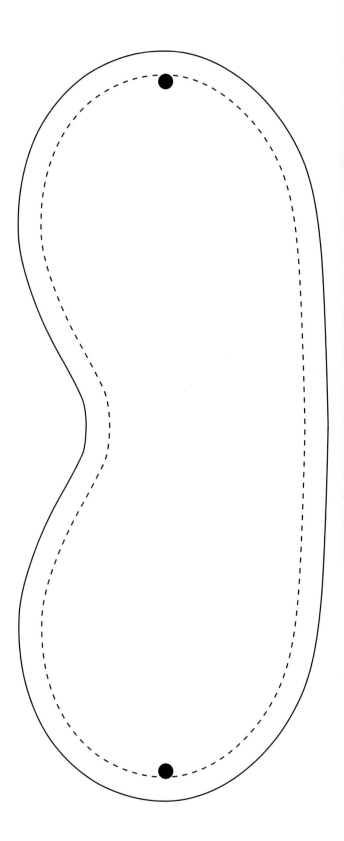

Comfort Roll

Yardage

Fat quarter muslin or cream fabric

Fat quarter violet fabric

1/2 yard 1" twill tape

3/4" x 4-3/4" strip of Velcro®

White rice, buckwheat, flax seed or old-fashioned oatmeal

Cutting

From the muslin fabric, cut: (1) 10-1/2" x 21-1/2" piece for inner pouch

From the violet fabric, cut: (1) 11" x 22" piece for outside cover

From the twill tape, cut: (2) 8" pieces

Sewing Instructions

1. Inner Pouch: Fold the 10-1/2" x 21-1/2" muslin piece in half lengthwise, right sides together. Sew ends and side together using a 1/2" seam allowance leaving a 2" opening along the long edge. Turn the muslin right side out. Fill inner pouch with rice to desired fullness. Stitch the opening closed.

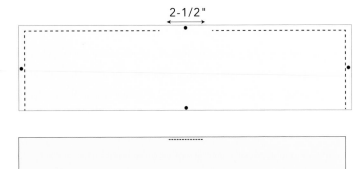

Note: Essential oils can be added to grain to enhance relaxation. Prepare grain with oils before putting in pouch.

2. Cover: Fold the 11" x 22" violet piece in half and mark the center. Fold the piece in half lengthwise and mark the center. Make a mark 2-1/2" on either side of center dot.

3. Position a raw edge of the twill tape on the 11" side of the violet piece, 3/4" in from the corner. Position the other end of the tape 3/4" away from center mark. Repeat for opposite end of the 11" piece as shown in the diagram. Baste tape edges to violet fabric.

4. Fold the 11" x 22" piece in half lengthwise, right sides together. Beginning at a mark 2-1/2" from the center, sew a 1/2" seam around the edge of the violet piece, stopping at the fold. Repeat on the opposite side. Turn the piece right side out. Press the seam allowance at opening. Place one side of the Velcro strip on the inside of cover on the seam allowance and stitch in place. Repeat with the remaining Velcro strip on the opposite seam allowance.

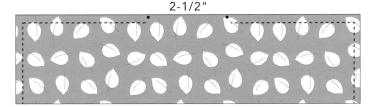

5. Place inner pouch in cover and close with Velcro.

Note: The inner pouch can be placed in the freezer to make a cold pack or in the microwave to make a hot pack. The cover can be removed and laundered as needed.

Carry All Tote

Cutting

From the grass green fabric, cut:
(2) 9-1/2" x 19" pieces

From the white-on-black fabric, cut:
(2) 3" x 19" pieces
(2) 2" x 29" pieces

From the teal fabric, cut:
(2) 12-1/2" x 19" pieces
(2) 3" x 19" pieces
(1) Base template on page 55

From the multi-check print fabric, cut:
(2) 13" x 31" pieces
(1) Base template on page 55

From the Pellon® Décor Bond®, cut:
(4) 3" x 19" pieces
(2) 9-1/2" x 19"   pieces
(1) Base template on page 55

From the Pellon® Peltex® Ultra-Firm iron on, cut:
(2) 12-1/2" x 19" pieces
(1) Base template on page 55

From the natural cording, cut:
(2) 18" lengths
(1) 36" length

Note: Put a piece of tape around the section of cording you are going to cut. Make the cut in the middle of tape. This will eliminate the cording expanding when handling it and pulling into handle strip.

From the 1/4"-wide elastic, cut:
(2) 19" lengths

WOF = width of fabric
Sew with a 1/2" seam allowance

Yardage

1/4 yard white-on-black fabric

1-1/4 yards teal fabric

7/8 yard multi-check print fabric

1 yard Pellon® Décor Bond

1 yard Pellon® Peltex® Single-sided
   Fusible Stabilizer

2 yards natural cording

1-1/8 yards 1/4"-wide elastic

4 1-1/2" grommets

Note: All seam allowances are 1/2" unless otherwise noted.

Sewing Instructions
Making the Outside Bag

1. Following manufacturer's directions, press the Décor Bond pieces to the wrong side of (2) 9-1/2"x 19" grass green pieces, (2) 3" x 19" white-on-black pieces, (2) 3" x 19" teal pieces and the teal base template piece.

2. Sew a 3" x 19" white-on-black piece to 3" x 19" teal piece, right sides together, along one long side. Press the seam open. Top stitch 1/8" on either side of the seam. Repeat with the remaining 3" x 19" white-on-black and teal pieces to make a total of 2 BC pieces.

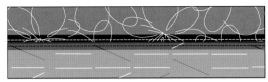

Make 2 BC pieces

3. Sew a 9-1/2" x 19" grass green piece to the white-on-black strip of the BC set, right sides together. Press seam open. Top stitch 1/8" on either side of the seam. Repeat with the remaining 9-1/2" x 19" grass green and BC pieces to make a total of 2 ABC sets.

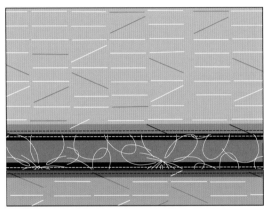

Make 2 ABC sets

4. Layer the 2 ABC sets right sides together, matching the side raw edges and seams. Sew the sets together on each side. Press seams open. Top stitch 1/8" along the side seams.

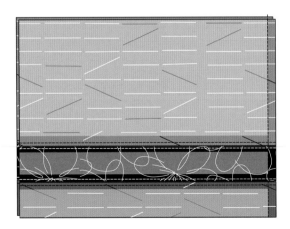

5. Fold the top edge of the grass green fabric over 1" to the wrong side of the fabric and finger press. Open the fold and place the 36"-length of natural cording in it. Start at a side seam and continue around the bag top, meeting back at the same side seam. Trim the end of the cording as necessary to butt up against the beginning of the cording. Place the top edge fold over the cording and pin in place.

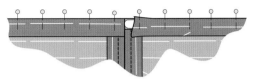

6. Positioning the sewing machine needle all the way to the right, or using a zipper foot, baste the fold in place on the inside of the bag close to the cording.

7. Fold the bag front/back in half by matching the side seams. Mark the folds on the top and bottom of the folds.

8. To mark the sides and middle of the teal base template piece, fold it in half lengthwise and mark each end of the fold. Fold the piece in half widthwise and mark each end of the fold.

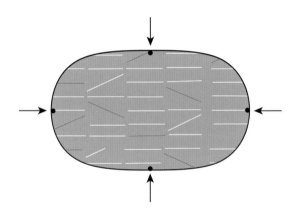

9. Position the bag, right sides together, with the teal base and teal bag bottom aligned. Match the bag's side seams to the marks on the short ends of the base template. Match the bag's side middle marks to the marks on the long edges of the base template.

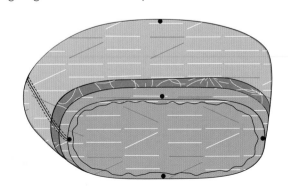

10. With the base piece on the bottom, sew a 1/2" seam around the base easing the bag sides around the curve and clipping when necessary. Trim the seam to 1/4".

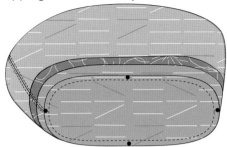

11. Turn bag right side out.

Making the Pockets

1. Fold a 13" x 31" multi-check print piece in half lengthwise and press. Sew 3/8" away from the folded edge to form a casing. Repeat with the remaining 13" x 31" multi-check print piece. These will be your pocket pieces with the casing at the top.

2. Fold a pocket piece in half and mark the top and bottom at the fold. Fold the piece in half again and mark the top and bottoms at the folds. Repeat with the remaining pocket piece.

3. Using a small safety pin, pull a 19"-length of elastic through the casing on each pocket piece. Secure at both edges.

Making the Bag Lining

1. Following manufacturer's directions, press the Peltex Ultra-Firm pieces to the wrong side of (2) 12-1/2" x 19" teal pieces and the multi-check print base template piece.

2. Fold a 12-1/2" x 19" teal piece in half and mark the top and bottom at the fold. Fold the piece in half again and mark the top and bottom at the folds. Repeat with the remaining 12-1/2" x 19" teal piece to make 2 lining pieces.

3. Place a pocket piece on the right side of a lining piece matching raw edges at the bottom corners and sides. Pin in place. Align the markings of the pockets and lining piece and pin in place along the bottom and top edge of each pocket.

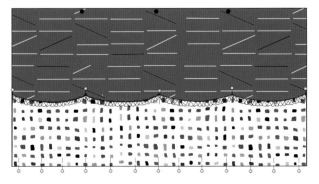

4. Sew a vertical seam from each pocket bottom mark to the top of the pocket piece to create sections. Backstitch at the top of the pocket to reinforce. Baste side seams in place.

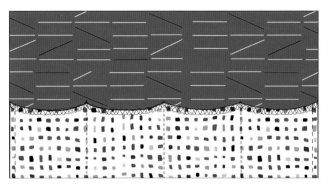

5. At each mark and at sides of pockets, fold the fabric in 3/4" toward the mark to create a pleat, pin in place. Make sure the side folds are 1/2" away from the raw edge. Baste along the bottom of the bag lining. Repeat for the remaining pocket and lining piece.

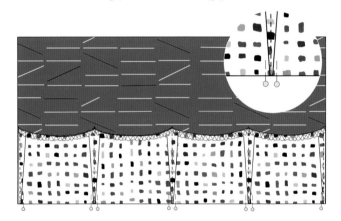

6. Layer the lining with pocket pieces right sides together. Sew the pieces together along each side. Press seams open.

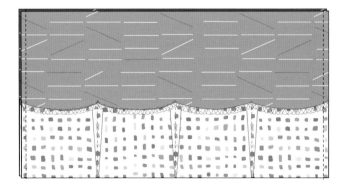

7. Referring to Outside Bag Assembly, steps 7-10, mark the centers on the multi-check print base template and sew to bag lining.

Bag Assembly

1. Place bag lining into the outer bag piece, wrong sides together. Matching the side seams and bottom pin the lining in place.

2. Fold over raw edge of the bag lining top approximately 1" to the wrong side of the fabric and finger press. Pin in place just below the cording on the inside of the bag.

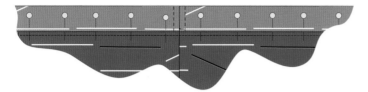

3. Positioning the sewing machine needle all the way to the right, or using a zipper foot, sew around bag top close to the folded edge of the lining just below the cording. Remove any previously sewn basting stitches.

Making the Handles

1. On the top and bottom of a 2" x 29" white-on-black piece, make a mark 6" from each end. Fold the strip in half lengthwise, right sides together, matching the top and bottom 6" marks on each end of the strip. Sew a 1/4" seam between the 6" marks. Press seam open, pressing a seam line fold all the way to the end of each strip. Turn the strip right side out.

2. Using a safety pin, pull an 18"-length of natural cording through the strip from step 1. Placement of cording will be 6" from the ends of the strip.

3. Fold in the ends of the strip 1/2" to the wrong side of the fabric. Fold the remaining open portion of the strip in half lengthwise, aligning the edges. To finish the bag handle, top stitch close to the folded edges to finish each end and secure in place. Make a total of 2 bag handles.

Finishing the Bag

1. Determine where you would like the grommets placed on the bag. Our grommets were placed approximately 5-1/4" from the side seams with approximately 4" between the outer edges of the grommets on each side of the bag.

2. After determining the placement of your grommets, measure 1-1/2" down from the top of the bag. This will be where you place the top of the grommet.

3. Following manufacturer's instructions, apply grommets to the bag.

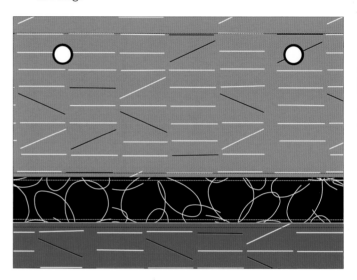

4. Pull one end of a bag handle through the front of a grommet. The handle's cording end should be even with the top of the grommet on the front of the bag. Pull the flat part of the handle through the grommet and create a small loop around the handle at the top of the bag. Tuck the end of the loop behind the flat strip and hand stitch in place to secure. Repeat with the other end of handle in the second grommet on the same side of the bag. Repeat with remaining handle on opposite side of the bag.

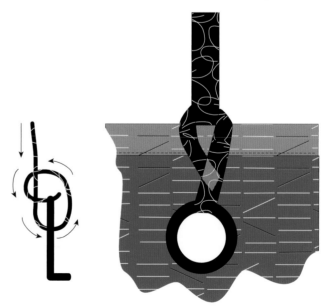

Bag Bottom Template

About Us

Our mom, Marilyn Johnson loved to sew. We are so lucky she passed this love to us. It has given us the opportunity to work together and weave our creativity and sewing passion into careers we love.

Our company, TailorMade by Design, focuses on creating designs and projects to highlight our textile clients' newest fabric collections. We also work to offer quilt shops and consumers patterns that inspire and challenge.

Acknowledgements

We have always said it is the people in the quilting industry that make our job so much fun. We are truly blessed to have an incredible group of ladies who piece and quilt for us. We simply could not create what we do without their commitment and willingness to work within our creative chaos! To find such delight in the creativity of fabric and to share this joy with such lovely ladies is absolutely the perfect Daily Zen.

Joanie   *Melanie*

Joanie and her husband Cody live south of Minneapolis in Farmington, Minnesota. Their children Zach (20) and Chloe (17) are their pride and joy.

Melanie and her husband RJ live in the country just north of Peoria, Illinois. They have three beautiful children, Olivia (22), Eli (19) and Emerson (15).

Visit the TailorMade by Design website at SewQuiltCraft.com.